★COFFEE★

Savor more than 85 coffee recipes

Publications International, Ltd.

Front cover photography and photography on page 19 by PIL Photo Studio North.

Pictured on the front cover (*clockwise from top left*): Banana Coffeecake (*page 54*), Espresso Gelato (*page 100*), Cream Cheese Brownie Royale (*page 66*) and Cinnamon Latte (*page 18*).

Pictured on the back cover (*top to bottom*): Glazed Cinnamon Coffeecake (*page 34*), Super-Easy Mocha Iced Chocolate Chip Cookies (*page 112*) and Toffee Coffee (*page 22*).

ISBN: 978-1-4508-9345-9

Library of Congress Control Number: 2014944757

Manufactured in China.

8 7 6 5 4 3 2 1

Microwave Cooking: Microwave ovens vary in wattage. Use the cooking times as guidelines and check for doneness before adding more time.

Preparation/Cooking Times: Preparation times are based on the approximate amount of time required to assemble the recipe before cooking, baking, chilling or serving. These times include preparation steps such as measuring, chopping and mixing. The fact that some preparations and cooking can be done simultaneously is taken into account. Preparation of optional ingredients and serving suggestions is not included.

CONTENTS

COFFEE HOUSE FAVORITES

MOCHA LATTE CHILLER

MAKES 1 SERVING

¼ cup milk

1 tablespoon chocolate syrup

½ cup brewed coffee

½ cup vanilla ice cream

Whipped topping and chocolate sprinkles (optional)

1. Combine milk and chocolate syrup in large glass. Pour in coffee; stir.

2. Add ice cream to coffee mixture. Top with whipped cream and sprinkles.

MINTY MOCHA: Substitute mint chocolate ice cream for the vanilla ice cream.

DOUBLE CHOCOLATE MOCHA: Substitute chocolate ice cream for the vanilla ice cream.

MALTED MOCHA: Substitute malt powder for the chocolate syrup.

SUGAR FREE ICED MOCHA

MAKES ABOUT 2 SERVINGS

¼ cup warm water

¼ cup fat-free half and half

2 tablespoons HERSHEY'S Cocoa

1 tablespoon powdered instant coffee

Sugar substitute with sweetening equivalence of 3 tablespoons sugar

1 teaspoon vanilla extract

1 cup ice

Additional ice

1. Place water, half and half, cocoa, instant coffee, sugar substitute and vanilla in blender container; cover and blend on low speed.

2. Add ice; cover and blend on high speed until smooth. Serve immediately over ice.

FROSTY FIVE-SPICE COFFEE SHAKE

MAKES 2 SERVINGS

⅔ cup vanilla ice cream

¼ cup sweetened condensed milk

2 tablespoons instant coffee granules

½ teaspoon Chinese five-spice powder

2 cups ice cubes

Whipped cream

1. Combine ice cream, condensed milk, coffee granules, five-spice powder and ice in blender; blend until smooth.

2. Pour into mugs; top with whipped cream. Serve immediately.

MUCHO MOCHA COCOA

MAKES 9 SERVINGS

1 cup chocolate syrup

⅓ cup instant coffee granules

2 tablespoons sugar

2 whole cinnamon sticks

1 quart whole milk

1 quart half-and-half

Slow Cooker Directions

Combine chocolate syrup, coffee granules, sugar, cinnamon sticks, milk and half-and-half in 3½- to 4-quart slow cooker; stir to blend. Cover; cook on LOW 3 hours. Remove and discard cinnamon sticks. Serve warm in mugs.

Frosty Five-Spice
Coffee Shake

CAPPUCCINO SMOOTHIE

MAKES 4 SERVINGS

1 can (12 fluid ounces) NESTLÉ® CARNATION® Evaporated Milk, *chilled*

5 to 6 teaspoons NESCAFÉ® TASTER'S CHOICE® Decaf House Blend 100% Pure Instant Coffee Granules

1 cup vanilla ice cream

1 cup ice cubes

1 tablespoon granulated sugar

2 teaspoons NESTLÉ® TOLL HOUSE® Baking Cocoa

PLACE evaporated milk and coffee granules in blender; cover. Blend until coffee is dissolved. Add ice cream, ice and sugar; blend until smooth. Pour into glasses. Sprinkle with cocoa.

PREP TIME: 10 minutes

MOCHA SUPREME

MAKES 8 SERVINGS

8 cups strong brewed coffee

½ cup instant hot chocolate mix

1 cinnamon stick, broken into halves

1 cup whipping cream

1 tablespoon powdered sugar

Slow Cooker Directions

1. Combine coffee and hot chocolate mix in 3- to 3½-quart slow cooker; stir until well blended. Add cinnamon stick halves. Cover; cook on HIGH 2 to 2½ hours.

2. Remove and discard cinnamon stick halves.

3. Beat cream in medium bowl with electric mixer on high speed until soft peaks form. Add powdered sugar; beat until stiff peaks form. Ladle coffee mixture into mugs; top with whipped cream.

NOTE: You can whip cream faster if you first chill the beaters and bowls in the freezer 15 minutes.

ICED COFFEE FRAPPÉ

MAKES 2 SERVINGS

1 cup strong brewed coffee, cooled

½ cup milk

2 tablespoons sugar

1 tablespoon chocolate syrup

Ice cubes

1. Combine coffee, milk, sugar, chocolate syrup and ice in blender or food processor; blend until smooth.

2. Pour into two glasses.

LUSCIOUS ALMOND MOCHA

MAKES 8 CUPS

½ cup HERSHEY'S SPECIAL DARK Cocoa

½ cup powdered instant coffee

1 cup sugar

1 cup hot water

6 cups milk

1 tablespoon vanilla extract

¼ to ½ teaspoon almond extract

Whipped topping (optional)

Additional cocoa

1. Whisk together first 4 ingredients in large saucepan until smooth. Bring to a boil over medium heat, whisking constantly. Boil 2 minutes, whisking constantly.

2. Add milk; cook to serving temperature. Do not boil. Stir in extracts. Serve in cups or mugs. Garnish with whipped topping, if desired; sift cocoa over top.

Iced Coffee Frappé

CHIPOTLE CHILI-SPIKED MOCHA SLUSH

MAKES 2 SERVINGS

1 package (1 to 1¼ ounces) instant hot chocolate mix without marshmallows

½ teaspoon instant coffee granules

⅛ teaspoon chipotle chili powder

⅛ teaspoon ground cinnamon plus additional for garnish

¾ cup hot water

1 cup coffee, vanilla or chocolate ice cream

⅓ cup half-and-half

Whipped cream and cinnamon sticks (optional)

1. Combine hot chocolate mix, coffee granules, chili powder and ⅛ teaspoon ground cinnamon in 2-cup glass measure. Stir in hot water until blended. Pour into ice cube tray. Freeze until firm.

2. Combine chocolate ice, ice cream and half-and-half in blender or food processor; blend until smooth.

3. Pour into two glasses. Garnish with whipped cream, additional ground cinnamon and cinnamon sticks. Serve immediately.

CINNAMON LATTE

MAKES 6 TO 8 SERVINGS

6 cups double-strength brewed coffee*

2 cups half-and-half

1 cup sugar

1 teaspoon vanilla

3 cinnamon sticks, plus additional for garnish

Double the amount of coffee grounds normally used to brew coffee. Or, substitute 8 teaspoons instant coffee dissolved in 6 cups boiling water.

Slow Cooker Directions

1. Combine coffee, half-and-half, sugar and vanilla in slow cooker; whisk to blend. Add 3 cinnamon sticks. Cover; cook on HIGH 3 hours.

2. Remove and discard cinnamon sticks. Serve latte in coffee mugs with additional cinnamon sticks, if desired.

HOT COCOA MOCHA

MAKES 3 TO 4 SERVINGS

¼ cup sugar

2 tablespoons HERSHEY'S Cocoa

2 tablespoons water

1 cup whipping cream

1¼ to 2 cups hot coffee

1. Stir together sugar and cocoa in microwave-safe 2-cup measure. Add water; stir until well blended. Microwave at HIGH (100%) 30 to 45 seconds or until mixture boils.

2. Add whipping cream; stir until well blended. Microwave at HIGH 1 to 1½ minutes or until hot. Combine cocoa mixture and coffee. Serve immediately.

Cinnamon Latte and
Banana Coffeecake (page 54)

MEXICAN COFFEE WITH CHOCOLATE AND CINNAMON

MAKES 10 TO 12 SERVINGS

6 cups water

½ cup ground dark roast coffee

2 cinnamon sticks

1 cup half-and-half

⅓ cup chocolate syrup

¼ cup packed dark brown sugar

1½ teaspoons vanilla, divided

1 cup whipping cream

¼ cup powdered sugar

Ground cinnamon

1. Place water in drip coffee maker. Place coffee and cinnamon sticks in coffee filter. Combine half-and-half, chocolate syrup, brown sugar and 1 teaspoon vanilla in coffee pot. Place coffee pot with cream mixture in coffee maker. Brew coffee; coffee will drip into chocolate cream mixture.

2. Meanwhile, beat whipping cream in medium bowl with electric mixer at high speed until soft peaks form. Add powdered sugar and remaining ½ teaspoon vanilla; beat until stiff peaks form.

3. Pour coffee into individual coffee cups; top with dollop of whipped cream. Sprinkle with ground cinnamon.

TOFFEE COFFEE

MAKES 4 SERVINGS

2 cups vanilla ice cream

½ cup milk

2 cups brewed coffee

1 cup ice cubes

½ cup chopped chocolate-covered toffee candy bar, divided

1. Combine ice cream, milk, coffee, ice and 6 tablespoons candy bar in blender; blend until smooth.

2. Pour into four glasses. Sprinkle evenly with remaining 2 tablespoons candy.

MOCHA SHAKE

MAKES 3 SERVINGS

¼ cup warm water

2 tablespoons HERSHEY'S Cocoa

1 tablespoon sugar

1 to 2 teaspoons powdered instant coffee

½ cup milk

2 cups vanilla ice cream

Place water, cocoa, sugar and instant coffee in blender container. Cover; blend briefly on low speed. Add milk. Cover; blend well on high speed. Add ice cream. Cover; blend until smooth. Garnish as desired. Serve immediately.

Toffee Coffee

MOCHA COOLER

MAKES 1 SERVING

1 cup milk

¼ cup coffee or vanilla
ice cream

1 tablespoon instant
coffee granules

1 tablespoon chocolate
syrup

1. Combine milk, ice cream, coffee granules and chocolate syrup in blender; blend until smooth.

2. Pour into glass.

TIP: Instant coffee granules are the result of removing water from brewed coffee through drying. It should be stored in a cool, dry place.

BREAKFAST MOCHA JAVA

MAKES 4 SERVINGS

3 cups milk

3 eggs

3 tablespoons sugar

3 tablespoons unsweetened cocoa powder

2 teaspoons instant decaffeinated coffee granules

1½ teaspoons vanilla

1. Combine milk, eggs, sugar, cocoa, coffee granules and vanilla in blender; blend until smooth.

2. Pour into four glasses. Serve immediately.

VARIATION: This rich and delicious shake tastes great served over ice, too.

ICED CAPPUCCINO

MAKES 6 SERVINGS

⅔ cup HERSHEY'S Syrup, chilled

2 cups cold coffee

2 cups vanilla ice cream

Ice cubes or crushed ice

Whipped topping (optional)

Ground cinnamon (optional)

1. Place syrup and coffee in blender container; cover and blend on high speed. Add ice cream; cover and blend until smooth.

2. Serve immediately over ice; top with whipped topping and ground cinnamon, if desired.

LOWER FAT ICED CAPPUCCINO: Follow above directions using reduced-fat vanilla ice cream and fat-free whipped topping.

Breakfast
Mocha
Java

VIENNESE COFFEE

MAKES 4 SERVINGS

3 cups strongly brewed coffee

3 tablespoons chocolate syrup

1 teaspoon sugar

⅓ cup whipping cream plus additional for garnish

¼ cup crème de cacao or Irish cream liqueur (optional)

Chocolate shavings (optional)

Slow Cooker Directions

1. Combine coffee, chocolate syrup and sugar in slow cooker. Cover; cook on LOW 2 to 2½ hours. Stir in ⅓ cup whipping cream and crème de cacao, if desired. Cover; cook on LOW 30 minutes or until heated through.

2. Ladle coffee into four coffee cups. Garnish with additional whipped cream and chocolate shavings, if desired.

TIP: The flavor of coffee can deteriorate very easily. Do not boil, reheat or leave it on a heating element for more than 15 minutes.

AMAZING COFFEECAKES

APPLE RING COFFEECAKE

MAKES 12 SERVINGS

3 cups all-purpose flour

1 teaspoon baking soda

1 teaspoon salt

1 teaspoon ground cinnamon

1 cup walnuts, chopped

1½ cups granulated sugar

1 cup vegetable oil

2 eggs

2 teaspoons vanilla

2 medium tart apples, peeled, cored and chopped

Powdered sugar (optional)

1. Preheat oven to 325°F. Grease 10-inch tube pan.

2. Sift flour, baking soda, salt and cinnamon into large bowl. Stir in walnuts; set aside.

3. Combine granulated sugar, oil, eggs and vanilla in medium bowl. Stir in apples. Stir into flour mixture just until moistened. Spoon batter evenly into prepared pan.

4. Bake 1 hour or until toothpick inserted into center comes out clean. Cool cake in pan on wire rack 10 minutes. Loosen edges with metal spatula, if necessary. Remove from pan; cool completely on wire rack.

5. Transfer to serving plate. Sprinkle with powdered sugar and serve immediately. Store leftover cake in airtight container.

PEANUT BUTTER COFFEE CAKE

MAKES 12 TO 16 SERVINGS

1⅔ cups (10-ounce package) REESE'S® Peanut Butter Chips

¾ cup REESE'S® Creamy Peanut Butter

2¼ cups all-purpose flour

1½ cups packed light brown sugar

½ cup (1 stick) butter or margarine, softened

1 teaspoon baking powder

½ teaspoon baking soda

1 cup milk

3 eggs

1 teaspoon vanilla extract

1. Heat oven to 350°F. Grease bottom of 13×9×2-inch baking pan.

2. Place peanut butter chips and peanut butter in microwave-safe bowl. Microwave at MEDIUM (50%) 1 minute; stir. If necessary, microwave at MEDIUM an additional 15 seconds at a time, stirring after each heating, just until chips are melted when stirred.

3. Combine flour, brown sugar, butter and peanut butter chip mixture in large bowl. Beat on low speed of mixer until mixture resembles small crumbs; reserve 1 cup crumbs. To remaining crumb mixture, gradually blend in baking powder, baking soda, milk, eggs and vanilla; beat until well combined. Pour batter into prepared pan; sprinkle with reserved crumbs.

4. Bake 35 to 40 minutes or until wooden pick inserted in center comes out clean. Cool completely in pan on wire rack.

GLAZED CINNAMON COFFEECAKE

MAKES 6 TO 8 SERVINGS

Streusel

- ¼ cup biscuit baking mix
- ¼ cup packed light brown sugar
- ½ teaspoon ground cinnamon

Batter

- 1½ cups biscuit baking mix
- ¾ cup granulated sugar
- ½ cup vanilla or plain yogurt
- 1 egg, lightly beaten
- 1 teaspoon vanilla

Glaze

- 1 to 2 tablespoons milk
- 1 cup powdered sugar
- ½ cup sliced almonds (optional)

Slow Cooker Directions

1. Coat inside of 4-quart slow cooker with butter or cooking spray. Cut parchment paper to fit bottom of stoneware* and press into place. Spray paper lightly with nonstick cooking spray.

2. For streusel, blend ¼ cup baking mix, brown sugar and cinnamon in small bowl; set aside.

3. For batter, mix 1½ cups baking mix, granulated sugar, yogurt, egg and vanilla in medium bowl until well blended. Spoon half of batter into slow cooker. Sprinkle half of streusel over top. Repeat with remaining batter and streusel.

4. Line lid with two paper towels. Cover; cook on HIGH 1¾ to 2 hours or until toothpick inserted into center comes out clean and cake springs back when gently touched. Allow cake to rest 10 minutes. Invert onto plate and peel off paper. Invert again onto serving plate.

NOTE: This recipe works best in a round slow cooker.

5. For glaze, whisk milk into powdered sugar in small bowl, 1 tablespoon at a time, until desired consistency. Spoon glaze over top of cake. Garnish with sliced almonds. Cut into wedges. Serve warm or cold.

*To cut parchment paper to fit, trace around the stoneware bottom, then cut the paper slightly smaller to fit. If parchment paper is unavailable, substitute waxed paper.

QUICK ALMOND OAT DANISH COFFEE CAKE

MAKES 8 SERVINGS

1 cup plus
2 tablespoons
QUAKER® Oats
(quick or old
fashioned, uncooked),
divided

5 tablespoons
margarine or butter,
melted

⅓ cup finely chopped
almonds

⅓ cup granulated sugar

2 tablespoons egg
substitute *or* 1 egg
white, lightly beaten,
divided

¾ teaspoon almond
extract

1 pound frozen bread
dough, thawed, at
room temperature

1 cup whole pitted
prunes or mixed dried
fruit

1. Spray cookie sheet with nonstick cooking spray or oil lightly.

2. Combine 1 cup oats and margarine in medium bowl; mix well. Stir in almonds, sugar, 1 tablespoon egg substitute and almond extract.

3. Turn bread dough out onto lightly floured surface. Roll or pat dough into 12×10-inch rectangle. Spread oat mixture in narrow strip down middle; top with prunes. On each side of filling, cut 3-inch diagonal slits 2 inches apart. Fold alternating strips of dough over filling to form a braid pattern, pinching ends of strips to seal. Transfer to prepared cookie sheet. Cover; let rise in warm place 30 minutes or until almost doubled in size.

4. Heat oven to 350°F. Brush loaf with remaining 1 tablespoon egg substitute; sprinkle with remaining 2 tablespoons oats.

5. Bake 30 to 35 minutes or until golden brown. Serve warm.

FRESH PLUM COFFEECAKE

MAKES 9 SERVINGS

2¼ cups all-purpose flour, divided

¼ cup packed brown sugar

½ teaspoon ground cinnamon

1 tablespoon butter, softened

1½ teaspoons baking powder

½ teaspoon baking soda

¼ teaspoon salt

1 cup lemon yogurt

⅔ cup granulated sugar

2 egg whites

1 egg

1 teaspoon grated lemon peel

4 medium plums, cut into ¼-inch-thick slices

1. Preheat oven to 350°F. Coat 9-inch square pan with nonstick cooking spray.

2. For topping, combine ¼ cup flour, brown sugar, cinnamon and butter in small bowl with fork until crumbs form; set aside.

3. Combine remaining 2 cups flour, baking powder, baking soda and salt in large bowl. Beat yogurt, granulated sugar, egg whites, egg and lemon peel in medium bowl with electric mixer 3 to 5 minutes or until well blended. Stir yogurt mixture into flour mixture just until ingredients are combined.

4. Pour batter into prepared pan. Arrange plums over batter; sprinkle evenly with reserved topping. Bake 30 to 35 minutes or until toothpick inserted into center of cake comes out clean. Cool in pan on wire rack. Serve warm or at room temperature.

CINNAMON WALNUT COFFEE CAKE

MAKES 12 TO 16 SERVINGS

¾ cup chopped walnuts

1 teaspoon ground cinnamon

1¼ cups sugar

1 cup (2 sticks) butter, softened

2 eggs

1 cup sour cream

1⅓ cups all-purpose flour

⅓ cup CREAM OF WHEAT® Cinnamon Swirl Instant Hot Cereal, uncooked

1½ teaspoons baking powder

½ teaspoon baking soda

1 teaspoon vanilla extract

1. Coat Bundt® pan with nonstick cooking spray. Sprinkle lightly with flour; shake out any excess. Combine walnuts and cinnamon in small bowl; set aside.

2. Cream sugar, butter and eggs in mixing bowl with electric mixer at medium speed. Add sour cream; blend well. Add flour, Cream of Wheat, baking powder and baking soda; mix well. Stir in vanilla. Sprinkle half of walnut mixture into bottom of prepared Bundt pan. Evenly spread half of batter over mixture. Sprinkle remaining walnut mixture over batter. Top with remaining batter, spreading evenly in Bundt pan.

3. Set oven to 350°F (do not preheat); place Bundt pan in cold oven. Bake 45 minutes or until toothpick inserted into center comes out clean. Remove from oven; let stand 5 minutes. Place serving plate over Bundt pan and turn pan over carefully onto plate; remove pan. Serve cake warm or cool.

PREP TIME: 15 minutes

START TO FINISH TIME: 1 hour

CHERRY-COCONUT-CHEESE COFFEECAKE

MAKES 10 SERVINGS

2½ cups all-purpose flour

¾ cup sugar

½ teaspoon baking powder

½ teaspoon baking soda

2 packages (3 ounces each) cream cheese, softened and divided

¾ cup milk

2 tablespoons vegetable oil

2 eggs, divided

1 teaspoon vanilla

½ cup flaked coconut

¾ cup cherry preserves

2 tablespoons butter

1. Preheat oven to 350°F. Grease and flour 9-inch springform pan. Combine flour and sugar in large bowl. Reserve ½ cup flour mixture; set aside. Stir baking powder and baking soda into remaining flour mixture. Cut in 1 package cream cheese with pastry blender or two knives until mixture resembles coarse crumbs; set aside.

2. Combine milk, oil and 1 egg in medium bowl. Add to cream cheese mixture; stir just until moistened. Spread batter on bottom and 1 inch up side of prepared pan. Combine remaining package cream cheese, remaining egg and vanilla in small bowl; stir until smooth. Pour over batter, spreading to within 1 inch of edge. Sprinkle coconut over cream cheese mixture. Spoon preserves evenly over coconut.

3. Cut butter into reserved flour mixture with pastry blender or two knives until mixture resembles coarse crumbs. Sprinkle over preserves.

4. Bake 55 to 60 minutes or until golden brown and toothpick inserted into center comes out clean. Cool in pan on wire rack 15 minutes. Remove side of pan; serve warm.

CLASSIC CARNATION® COFFEECAKE

MAKES 12 SERVINGS

2½ cups all-purpose baking mix

½ cup dry NESTLÉ® CARNATION® Instant Nonfat Dry Milk

⅓ cup plus 1 tablespoon butter, softened

½ cup packed brown sugar, *divided*

¼ cup plus 2 tablespoons granulated sugar, *divided*

3 large eggs

½ cup water

1 teaspoon ground cinnamon

PREHEAT oven to 350°F. Grease 9-inch-square baking pan.

COMBINE baking mix and dry milk in small bowl. Beat *⅓ cup* butter, *¼ cup* brown sugar and *¼ cup* granulated sugar in large mixer bowl until creamy. Add eggs and water; beat on medium speed for 2 minutes until blended. Gradually beat in baking mix mixture just until blended.

COMBINE *remaining ¼ cup* brown sugar, *2 tablespoons* granulated sugar, *1 tablespoon* butter and cinnamon in small bowl.

SPREAD batter into prepared pan. Sprinkle cinnamon-sugar mixture over batter. Poke round end of wooden spoon randomly into batter to form streusel ribbons in cake.

BAKE for 30 to 35 minutes or until wooden pick inserted in center comes out clean. Cool in pan on wire rack. Serve warm. Store any remaining cake tightly covered.

PREP TIME: 20 minutes

BAKING TIME: 30 minutes

GINGERBREAD COFFEECAKE

MAKES 10 SERVINGS

2 tablespoons finely chopped walnuts

½ cup plus 2 tablespoons packed dark brown sugar, divided

⅔ cup whole wheat flour

¼ cup all-purpose flour

¼ cup granulated sugar

3 to 4 teaspoons ground ginger

1½ teaspoons baking powder

1 teaspoon ground cinnamon

½ teaspoon salt

½ teaspoon ground cloves

¼ teaspoon baking soda

½ cup prune purée

2 eggs

1 cup buttermilk

2 tablespoons canola oil

1 teaspoon vanilla

Whipped topping (optional)

1. Preheat oven to 350°F. Spray 9-inch round cake pan with nonstick cooking spray; set aside. Combine walnuts and 2 tablespoons brown sugar in small bowl. Set aside.

2. Combine remaining ½ cup brown sugar, flours, granulated sugar, ginger, baking powder, cinnamon, salt, cloves and baking soda in large bowl; set aside.

3. Combine prune purée and eggs in medium bowl. Whisk in buttermilk, oil and vanilla. Add buttermilk mixture to flour mixture; stir just until combined. Pour into prepared pan. Sprinkle with reserved walnut mixture.

4. Bake 25 to 30 minutes or until toothpick inserted into center comes out clean. Serve with whipped topping, if desired.

LITTLE CHOCOLATE CHIP COFFEECAKES

MAKES 18 COFFEECAKES

1⅓ cups all-purpose flour

¾ teaspoon baking powder

½ teaspoon salt

¼ teaspoon baking soda

¾ cup packed brown sugar

½ cup (1 stick) butter, softened

¼ cup granulated sugar

1 teaspoon vanilla

2 eggs

½ cup plus 3 tablespoons milk, divided

1½ cups semisweet chocolate chips, divided

1. Preheat oven to 350°F. Generously grease and flour 18 mini (¼-cup) bundt cups. Combine flour, baking powder, salt and baking soda in small bowl.

2. Beat brown sugar, butter, granulated sugar and vanilla in large bowl with electric mixer at medium speed until light and fluffy. Beat in eggs, one at a time, until well blended. Alternately add flour mixture and ½ cup milk, beginning and ending with flour mixture; beat at low speed until blended. Stir in 1 cup chocolate chips.

3. Spoon batter into prepared bundt cups, filling three-fourths full (about 3 tablespoons batter per cup).

4. Bake 16 minutes or until toothpick inserted into centers comes out clean. Cool cakes in pans 5 minutes; invert onto wire racks to cool completely.

5. Combine remaining ½ cup chocolate chips and 3 tablespoons milk in small microwavable bowl. Microwave on HIGH 30 seconds; stir. Microwave at 15-second intervals until chocolate is melted and mixture is smooth. Drizzle glaze over cakes.

APRICOT SPICE COFFEECAKE

MAKES 10 SERVINGS

1 cup whole wheat flour

½ teaspoon baking soda

½ teaspoon ground cinnamon

¼ teaspoon salt

½ cup buttermilk

¼ cup packed brown sugar

2 tablespoons canola oil

1 egg

1 teaspoon vanilla

1 can (15 ounces) apricot halves in juice, drained

1 tablespoon old-fashioned oats

¼ cup powdered sugar

1 to 2 teaspoons milk

1. Preheat oven to 350°F. Spray 8- or 9-inch round cake pan with nonstick cooking spray.

2. Combine flour, baking soda, cinnamon and salt in small bowl; mix well. Whisk buttermilk, brown sugar, oil, egg and vanilla in large bowl until smooth and well blended. Stir in flour mixture just until moistened. Pour batter into prepared pan. Arrange apricot halves, cut side down, over batter. Sprinkle evenly with oats.

3. Bake 27 to 30 minutes or until golden brown and top springs back when touched in center. Cool in pan on wire rack 10 minutes.

4. Whisk powdered sugar and 1 teaspoon milk in small bowl until blended. Add additional milk, if necessary, until desired consistency is reached. Drizzle over coffeecake. Serve warm.

PINEAPPLE COFFEE CAKE

MAKES 8 SERVINGS

1 can (20 ounces) DOLE® Pineapple Chunks

½ cup packed brown sugar

1 teaspoon ground cinnamon

½ cup chopped walnuts

3 tablespoons butter or margarine, diced

2 cups prepared baking mix

2 tablespoons granulated sugar

1 egg

- Drain pineapple, reserve ⅔ cup juice. Pat pineapple dry.

- Mix brown sugar, cinnamon, walnuts and butter in medium bowl; set aside.

- Beat reserved juice with baking mix, granulated sugar and egg in large bowl for 30 seconds. Spoon into 9-inch round baking pan sprayed with nonstick vegetable cooking spray. Top with half of walnut mixture, pineapple and remaining walnut mixture.

- Bake at 400°F., 20 to 25 minutes. Cool.

PREP TIME: 20 minutes

BAKING TIME: 25 minutes

BANANA COFFEECAKE

MAKES 9 SERVINGS

½ cup 100% bran cereal

½ cup strong brewed coffee

1 cup mashed ripe bananas (about 2 bananas)

½ cup sugar

1 egg, lightly beaten

2 tablespoons canola or vegetable oil

½ cup all-purpose flour

½ cup whole wheat flour

2 teaspoons baking powder

1 teaspoon ground cinnamon

¼ teaspoon salt

1. Preheat oven to 350°F. Coat 8-inch square baking dish with nonstick cooking spray; set aside.

2. Combine cereal and coffee in large bowl; let stand 3 minutes or until cereal softens. Stir in bananas, sugar, egg and oil.

3. Combine all-purpose flour, whole wheat flour, baking powder, cinnamon and salt in small bowl; stir into banana mixture just until moistened. Pour into prepared pan.

4. Bake 25 to 35 minutes or until toothpick inserted into center of cake comes out clean. Cool in pan on wire rack. Cut into nine squares before serving.

BLUEBERRY POPPY SEED COFFEECAKE

MAKES 8 SERVINGS

1½ cups all-purpose flour

½ cup sugar

1 teaspoon baking powder

½ teaspoon baking soda

¼ teaspoon salt

¼ cup (½ stick) cold butter, cut into small pieces

1 tablespoon poppy seeds

¾ cup buttermilk

1 egg

1 teaspoon vanilla

1 teaspoon grated lemon peel

1 cup fresh blueberries

1. Preheat oven to 350°F. Spray 9-inch round cake pan with nonstick cooking spray; set aside.

2. Combine flour, sugar, baking powder, baking soda and salt in large bowl. Cut in butter using pastry blender or two knives until mixture resembles coarse crumbs. Stir in poppy seeds.

3. Whisk buttermilk, egg, vanilla and lemon peel in small bowl until blended. Stir buttermilk mixture into flour mixture just until flour mixture is moistened. Spread half of batter into prepared pan; top with blueberries. Drop remaining batter in eight dollops onto blueberries, leaving some berries uncovered.

4. Bake 33 to 36 minutes or until top is golden brown. Cool 15 minutes in pan on wire rack. Serve warm.

BROWNIES AND BARS

COFFEE BROWNIE BITES

MAKES 5 DOZEN BROWNIES

1 package (21 ounces) fudge brownie mix

3 eggs

½ cup vegetable oil

2 teaspoons instant coffee granules

2 teaspoons coffee liqueur (optional)

Powdered sugar

1. Preheat oven to 325°F. Lightly spray 60 mini (1¾-inch) muffin cups with nonstick cooking spray.

2. Combine brownie mix, eggs, oil, coffee granules and coffee liqueur, if desired, in medium bowl; stir until well blended.

3. Fill each cup with 1 tablespoon brownie mixture. Bake 13 minutes or until toothpick inserted into centers comes out almost clean.

4. Remove to wire rack; cool completely. Sprinkle with powdered sugar. Store in airtight container.

GLAZED MOCHA BROWNIES

MAKES 16 BROWNIES

¾ cup (1½ sticks) plus 1 tablespoon unsalted butter, cut into small pieces and divided

1 cup milk chocolate chips

1 cup coarsely chopped pecans

2 bars (3.5 ounces each) coffee-flavored dark chocolate,* broken into pieces and divided

¾ cup all-purpose flour

½ cup granulated sugar

⅓ cup packed dark brown sugar

¼ teaspoon salt

3 eggs

1 tablespoon whipping cream

Flavored dark chocolate bars can be found in the supermarket gourmet candy section.

1. Preheat oven to 350°F. Spray 8-inch baking pan with nonstick cooking spray.

2. Heat ¾ cup butter in top of double boiler over low heat, stirring occasionally until melted. Add chocolate chips, pecans, half of dark chocolate pieces, flour, granulated sugar, brown sugar and salt; cook and stir until chocolate is melted and mixture forms batter. Remove from heat. Add eggs, one at a time, beating well after each addition. Spoon into prepared pan.

3. Bake 30 to 35 minutes or until edges start to pull away from pan and top is firm to the touch. Cool completely in pan on wire rack.

4. Place remaining half of chocolate pieces, whipping cream and remaining 1 tablespoon butter in top of double boiler over simmering water. Stir constantly until chocolate is melted. Spread evenly over brownies. Allow glaze to set 2 hours. Cut into bars.

NOTE: These brownies become much fudgier if you let them stand for a few hours or overnight.

COCONUT CROWNED BROWNIES

MAKES 16 BROWNIES

- 6 squares (1 ounce each) semisweet chocolate, coarsely chopped
- 1 tablespoon instant coffee granules
- 1 tablespoon boiling water
- ½ cup sugar
- ¼ cup (½ stick) butter, softened
- 3 eggs, divided
- ¾ cup all-purpose flour
- ¾ teaspoon ground cinnamon
- ½ teaspoon baking powder
- ¼ teaspoon salt
- ¼ cup whipping cream
- 1 teaspoon vanilla
- ¾ cup flaked coconut, toasted and divided*
- ½ cup semisweet chocolate chips, divided

*To toast coconut, spread in a thin layer on small baking sheet. Bake at 325°F 10 minutes or until golden brown.

1. Preheat oven to 350°F. Grease 8-inch square baking pan. Melt chocolate squares in small, heavy saucepan over low heat, stirring constantly; set aside. Dissolve coffee granules in boiling water in small cup; set aside.

2. Beat sugar and butter in large bowl until light and fluffy. Beat in 2 eggs, one at a time, scraping down side of bowl after each addition. Beat in chocolate and coffee mixtures until well blended. Combine flour, cinnamon, baking powder and salt in small bowl; add to butter mixture. Beat until well blended. Spread evenly in prepared pan.

3. Combine whipping cream, remaining egg and vanilla in small bowl; blend well. Stir in ½ cup coconut and ¼ cup chocolate chips. Spread evenly over brownie batter; sprinkle with remaining ¼ cup coconut and ¼ cup chocolate chips.

4. Bake 30 to 35 minutes or until coconut is browned and center is set. Remove pan to wire rack; cool completely. Cut into 2-inch squares.

NORMA'S COCOA BROWNIES

MAKES ABOUT 30 BROWNIES

2 cups all-purpose flour

2 cups granulated
sugar

1 cup (2 sticks) butter

1 cup hot coffee

¼ cup unsweetened
cocoa powder

½ cup buttermilk

2 eggs, lightly beaten

1 teaspoon baking soda

1 teaspoon vanilla

Cocoa Frosting
(recipe follows)

1. Preheat oven to 400°F. Butter 17½×11-inch jelly-roll pan.

2. Combine flour and granulated sugar in large bowl. Combine butter, coffee and cocoa in small, heavy saucepan. Bring to a boil over medium heat, stirring constantly. Combine buttermilk, eggs, baking soda and vanilla in small bowl. Stir cocoa mixture into flour mixture until smooth. Stir in buttermilk mixture until well blended. Pour batter into prepared pan.

3. Bake 20 minutes or until center springs back when touched.

4. Meanwhile, prepare Cocoa Frosting. Remove brownies from oven. Immediately pour warm frosting over hot brownies, spreading evenly. Cool in pan on wire rack. Cut into 2½-inch squares.

COCOA FROSTING

MAKES ABOUT 3 CUPS

½ cup (1 stick) butter

2 tablespoons
unsweetened cocoa
powder

¼ cup milk

3½ cups powdered sugar

1 teaspoon vanilla

Combine butter, cocoa and milk in large saucepan. Bring to a boil over medium heat. Remove from heat. Stir in powdered sugar and vanilla; beat until smooth.

CREAM CHEESE BROWNIE ROYALE

MAKES 16 SERVINGS

1 package (about 15 ounces) brownie mix

⅔ cup cold coffee

1 package (8 ounces) cream cheese, softened

1 egg

2 tablespoons sugar

1 tablespoon milk

½ teaspoon vanilla

1. Preheat oven to 350°F. Spray 13×9-inch baking pan with nonstick cooking spray.

2. Combine brownie mix and coffee in large bowl; stir until blended. Spread brownie mixture evenly into prepared pan.

3. Beat cream cheese, egg, sugar, milk and vanilla in medium bowl with electric mixer at medium speed until smooth. Spoon cream cheese mixture in small dollops over brownie mixture. Swirl cream cheese mixture into brownie mixture with tip of knife.

4. Bake 30 to 35 minutes or until toothpick inserted into center comes out clean. Cool completely in pan on wire rack.

5. Cover with foil and refrigerate 8 hours or until ready to serve. Cut into 16 squares.

SIMPLY SPECIAL BROWNIES

MAKES 20 BROWNIES

½ cup (1 stick) butter or margarine

1 package (4 ounces) HERSHEY'S Semi-Sweet Chocolate Baking Bar, broken into pieces

2 eggs

1 teaspoon vanilla extract

¾ teaspoon powdered instant coffee

⅔ cup sugar

½ cup all-purpose flour

¼ teaspoon baking soda

¼ teaspoon salt

½ cup coarsely chopped nuts

1. Heat oven to 350°F. Grease 9-inch square baking pan.

2. Place butter and chocolate in medium microwave-safe bowl. Microwave at MEDIUM (50%) 1 minute; stir. If necessary, microwave an additional 15 seconds at a time, stirring after each heating, until chocolate is melted and mixture is smooth when stirred. Add eggs, vanilla and instant coffee, stirring until well blended. Stir in sugar, flour, baking soda and salt; blend completely. Stir in nuts. Spread batter in prepared pan.

3. Bake 25 to 30 minutes or until wooden pick inserted in center comes out almost clean. Cool completely in pan on wire rack. Cut into bars.

PREP TIME: 10 minutes

COOK TIME: 25 minutes

MOCHA CREAM CHEESE MOUSSE BROWNIES

MAKES 2 DOZEN BROWNIES

1 package (about 19 ounces) brownie mix

½ cup vegetable oil

2 eggs

¼ cup water

1½ tablespoons instant coffee granules, divided

4 ounces cream cheese, softened

1 cup powdered sugar

¼ cup unsweetened cocoa powder

1 teaspoon vanilla

1 container (8 ounces) frozen whipped topping, thawed

¼ recipe Chocolate Ganache (page 71)

1. Preheat oven to 350°F. Spray 13×9-inch baking pan with nonstick cooking spray.

2. Combine brownie mix, oil, eggs, water and 1½ teaspoons coffee granules in medium bowl. Mix according to package directions. Spread batter in prepared pan. Bake 26 to 28 minutes or until toothpick inserted 1 inch from edge comes out clean. Cool completely in pan on wire rack.

3. Meanwhile, mix cream cheese, powdered sugar, cocoa, vanilla and remaining 3 teaspoons coffee granules in medium bowl until smooth. Fold in whipped topping. Cover with plastic wrap; refrigerate until needed.

4. Spread mousse topping evenly over brownies. Prepare Chocolate Ganache. Pour warm Chocolate Ganache into medium food storage bag; seal bag. Cut small hole from one corner. Pipe lines of Chocolate Ganache over mousse. Drag toothpick or paring knife through Chocolate Ganache to create design, if desired. Refrigerate until well chilled. Cut into bars. Store covered in refrigerator.

CHOCOLATE GANACHE: Heat 1 cup whipping cream and 2 tablespoons butter in medium saucepan over medium heat until warm. (Do not boil.) Remove from heat. Add 1 cup semisweet chocolate chips; let stand 1 minute. Stir until smooth. Refrigerate leftovers. Makes 2 cups.

JAVA CREAM BROWNIE BARS

MAKES 16 BARS

1 package (about 19 ounces) brownie mix, plus ingredients to prepare mix

¼ cup raspberry fruit spread

1 cup whipping cream, divided

4 ounces semisweet chocolate chips

1 teaspoon instant coffee granules

¼ cup powdered sugar

1. Preheat oven to 350°F. Line 9-inch square baking pan with double layer of foil, allowing 2-inch overhang around all sides.

2. Prepare brownie mix according to package directions; pour batter into prepared pan. Bake 35 minutes or until toothpick inserted into center comes out clean. Cool completely in pan on wire rack.

3. Melt fruit spread in medium saucepan over medium heat, stirring frequently. Brush evenly over cooled brownies. Bring ½ cup cream to a simmer in same saucepan over medium heat. (Do not boil.) Remove from heat; stir in chocolate chips until melted and smooth. Pour chocolate mixure evenly over top; let cool.

4. Combine 2 tablespoons cream and coffee granules; stir until completely dissolved. Beat remaining 6 tablespoons cream in medium bowl with electric mixer at medium-high speed until soft peaks form. Gradually add coffee mixture and powdered sugar; beat until stiff peaks form. Spread over brownies. Refrigerate until ready to serve. Lift brownies out of pan using foil edges; peel back foil. Cut into 3×1½-inch bars.

CHEERY CHOCOLATE-CHERRY BROWNIES

MAKES 16 BROWNIES

¾ cup (1½ sticks) unsalted butter, melted and cooled

2 eggs, at room temperature

1 teaspoon vanilla

1 cup granulated sugar

1 cup unsweetened cocoa powder

¾ cup all-purpose flour

¼ cup packed light brown sugar

2 teaspoons instant espresso powder or coffee granules

½ teaspoon baking powder

¼ teaspoon salt

1 cup chocolate-covered cherries*

Powdered sugar

*If unavailable, substitute dried cherries.

1. Preheat oven to 350°F. Spray 8-inch baking pan with nonstick cooking spray.

2. Combine butter, eggs and vanilla in large bowl. Add granulated sugar, cocoa, flour, brown sugar, espresso powder, baking powder and salt; stir until blended. Stir in cherries. Spread batter evenly into prepared pan.

3. Bake 28 to 30 minutes or until toothpick inserted into center comes out clean. Cool completely in pan on wire rack. Sprinkle with powdered sugar. Cut into bars.

RASPBERRY-GLAZED BROWNIES WITH CHEESECAKE TOPPING

MAKES 12 SERVINGS

¾ cup all-purpose flour

9 tablespoons sugar, divided

¼ cup unsweetened cocoa powder

¾ teaspoon baking powder

⅛ teaspoon salt

1 jar (2½ ounces) prune purée

¼ cup cold coffee

1 egg

2 tablespoons canola oil

¾ teaspoon vanilla, divided

¼ cup seedless raspberry fruit spread

2 ounces cream cheese, softened

4½ teaspoons milk

1. Preheat oven to 350°F.

2. Combine flour, 7 tablespoons sugar, cocoa, baking powder and salt in large bowl; stir until blended. Combine prune purée, coffee, egg, oil and ½ teaspoon vanilla in medium bowl; stir until well blended. Make well in center of dry ingredients; add prune purée mixture. Stir until just blended.

3. Spread batter evenly in ungreased 8-inch square nonstick baking pan. Bake 8 minutes. (Brownies will not appear to be done.) Cool completely in pan on wire rack.

4. Meanwhile, place raspberry spread in small microwavable bowl. Microwave on HIGH 10 seconds; stir until smooth. Brush evenly over brownies with pastry brush.

5. Combine cream cheese, milk, remaining 2 tablespoons sugar and ¼ teaspoon vanilla in medium bowl. Beat at medium speed with electric mixer until well blended and smooth.

6. Cut brownies into 12 rectangles; top with dollops of cream cheese mixture.

PHARAOH'S GOLD

MAKES 32 BROWNIES

1 package (19 to 21 ounces) fudge brownie mix

¼ cup coffee

½ cup vegetable oil

2 eggs

½ cup pecan pieces

1 cup sweetened flaked coconut

1 container (16 ounces) dark chocolate fudge frosting

1 cup mini marshmallows

½ cup mini candy-coated plain chocolate candies

¼ cup butterscotch or caramel ice cream topping

1. Preheat oven to 350°F. Spray 13×9-inch nonstick baking pan with nonstick cooking spray.

2. Combine brownie mix, coffee, oil and eggs in medium bowl; stir until well blended. Spread in prepared pan.

3. Bake 28 minutes or until toothpick inserted 2 inches from side of pan comes out almost clean. Cool completely in pan on wire rack.

4. Meanwhile, place nuts in single layer on foil-lined baking sheet. Bake 5 minutes or until just brown. Remove and set aside.

5. Place coconut in single layer on a foil-lined baking sheet. Bake 2 minutes. Stir. Bake 1 minute or until just golden.

6. Spread frosting evenly over brownies. Sprinkle with marshmallows, nuts and candy pieces. Drizzle ice cream topping over all. Sprinkle with coconut. Cut and store in airtight container up to three days.

CHOCOLATE ESPRESSO BROWNIES

MAKES 36 BROWNIES

4 squares (1 ounce each) unsweetened chocolate

1 cup sugar

¼ cup Dried Plum Purée (recipe follows) or prepared dried plum butter

3 egg whites

1 to 2 tablespoons instant espresso coffee powder

1 teaspoon baking powder

1 teaspoon salt

1 teaspoon vanilla

½ cup all-purpose flour

Powdered sugar

Preheat oven to 350°F. Coat 8-inch square baking pan with vegetable cooking spray. In small heavy saucepan, melt chocolate over very low heat, stirring until melted and smooth. Remove from heat; cool. In mixer bowl, beat chocolate and remaining ingredients except flour and powdered sugar at medium speed until well blended; mix in flour. Spread batter evenly in prepared pan. Bake in center of oven about 30 minutes until pick inserted into center comes out clean. Cool completely in pan on wire rack. Dust with powdered sugar. Cut into 1⅓-inch squares.

DRIED PLUM PURÉE: Combine 1⅓ cups (8 ounces) pitted dried plums and 6 tablespoons hot water in container of food processor or blender. Pulse on and off until dried plums are finely chopped and smooth. Store leftovers in a covered container in the refrigerator for up to two months. Makes 1 cup.

*Favorite Recipe from **California Dried Plum Board***

WORLDWIDE SPECIALTIES

COFFEE GRANITA

MAKES 5 SERVINGS

2 cups water

1½ tablespoons instant coffee granules

¼ cup powdered sugar

2 tablespoons granulated sugar

1. Combine water, coffee granules, powdered sugar and granulated sugar in small saucepan. Bring to a boil over medium-high heat, stirring until coffee and sugars are dissolved completely.

2. Pour into metal 8-inch square pan. Cover with foil; freeze granita 2 hours or until slushy. Remove from freezer and stir to break mixture up into small chunks. Cover; return to freezer. Freeze 2 hours then stir to break granita up. Cover; freeze 4 hours or overnight.

3. To serve, scrape surface of granita with large metal spoon to shave off thin pieces. Spoon into individual bowls. Serve immediately.

MINI TIRAMISÙ CUPCAKES

MAKES 18 CUPCAKES

2 teaspoons instant espresso powder

1 tablespoon hot water

1 tablespoon coffee liqueur

1 package (about 18 ounces) butter recipe yellow cake mix

3 eggs

⅔ cup water

½ cup (1 stick) butter, softened and cut into small pieces

1 package (8 ounces) mascarpone cheese*

½ cup powdered sugar

¼ teaspoon vanilla

½ (8-ounce) container French vanilla whipped topping

Unsweetened cocoa powder

Mascarpone cheese is an Italian soft cheese (similar to cream cheese) that is a traditional ingredient in tiramisu. Look for it in the specialty cheese section of the supermarket.

1. Preheat oven to 350°F. Line 18 standard (2½-inch) muffin cups with paper baking cups. Stir espresso powder into hot water in medium bowl until dissolved. Add liqueur; mix well.

2. Beat cake mix, eggs, water and butter in large bowl with electric mixer at medium speed 3 minutes or until smooth. Remove half of batter to coffee mixture; mix well. Spoon equal amounts of coffee and plain batters into each prepared muffin cup, filling three-fourths full. Swirl batters with toothpick or paring knife.

3. Bake 16 to 18 minutes or until toothpick inserted into centers comes out clean. Cool in pans 10 minutes. Remove to wire racks; cool completely.

4. For filling, combine mascarpone cheese, powdered sugar and vanilla in medium bowl. Fold in whipped topping.

5. Cut off tops of cupcakes; cut out designs in center of cupcake tops with mini cookie cutters.

6. Spoon filling evenly over cupcake bottoms. Sprinkle cupcake tops with cocoa; place over filling. Refrigerate 2 hours before serving.

INDIVIDUAL IRISH COFFEE BAKED ALASKA

MAKES 4 SERVINGS

2 cups vanilla ice
cream, softened

2 cups coffee ice
cream, softened

Cake

⅔ cup sugar

3 eggs, separated

⅓ cup all-purpose flour

⅓ cup unsweetened
cocoa powder

¼ cup cornstarch

2 tablespoons Irish
cream-flavored
liqueur

Meringue

4 egg whites

½ cup sugar

3 tablespoons whiskey

1. Preheat oven to 350°F. Line 4 (1-cup) ramekins with plastic wrap. Place ½ cup vanilla ice cream in each ramekin. Top with ½ cup coffee ice cream. Fold plastic down on top of ice cream. Freeze 4 hours or until firm.

2. For cake, line 13×9-inch baking pan with waxed paper. Beat sugar and egg yolks in medium bowl with electric mixer at high speed 4 minutes or until pale and thick; set aside. Beat egg whites in clean bowl at high speed until stiff peaks form. Sift flour, cocoa and cornstarch into yolk mixture; stir gently until blended. Fold in egg whites. Carefully spread mixture into prepared baking pan.

3. Bake 10 minutes or until cake springs back lightly when touched. Cool completely in pan on wire rack. Cut cake into 3-inch rounds with cookie or biscuit cutter. Place rounds on top of ice cream in ramekins. Brush rounds with liqueur. Freeze until ready to top with meringue.

4. For meringue, preheat oven to 525°F. Beat egg whites in clean medium bowl with electric mixer at high speed until foamy. Slowly add sugar, beating until stiff, glossy peaks form.

5. Remove desserts from ramekins using plastic wrap. Discard plastic wrap. Place desserts, cake side down, on baking sheet. Spread ⅔ cup meringue over each dessert, working quickly to prevent ice cream from melting. Bake 2 minutes or until meringue is golden.

6. Heat whiskey in small skillet over low heat 1 minute. *Do not boil.* Using long-handled match, ignite whiskey. Carefully pour over each dessert. Allow whiskey to burn out; serve immediately.

AZTEC BROWNIES

MAKES 18 TO 24 BROWNIES

1 **package (12 ounces) semisweet chocolate chips**

1 **cup (2 sticks) butter, softened**

1 **cup sugar**

3 **eggs**

1 **tablespoon instant coffee granules or powder**

1 **tablespoon vanilla**

¾ **cup all-purpose flour**

2 **teaspoons baking powder**

1 **teaspoon ground cinnamon**

1 **to 2 teaspoons chili powder**

½ **teaspoon salt**

¾ **cup sliced almonds**

1. Preheat oven to 350°F. Spray 13×9-inch baking pan with nonstick cooking spray. Line pan with foil; spray foil.

2. Place chocolate chips and butter in medium microwavable bowl; microwave on HIGH 30 seconds. Stir until mixture is smooth. (If lumps remain, microwave 10 seconds more and stir again.)

3. Whisk sugar, eggs, coffee granules and vanilla in medium bowl until well blended. Stir in warm chocolate mixture; set aside to cool 10 minutes. Whisk flour, baking powder, cinnamon, chili powder and salt in large bowl; stir in chocolate mixture until well blended. Pour into prepared pan.

4. Bake 15 minutes; remove pan from oven and sprinkle with almonds. Bake 20 minutes or until top is no longer shiny and toothpick inserted into center comes out almost clean. *Do not overbake.* Cool completely in pan on wire rack before cutting into triangles.

TIP: For easier cutting, refrigerate the brownies a few hours before cutting.

HAZELNUT CAPPUCCINO RUGALACH

MAKES 64 PIECES

1 **package (17.3 ounces) PEPPERIDGE FARM® Puff Pastry Sheets (2 sheets)**

¾ **cup sugar**

2 **tablespoons cappuccino coffee drink mix**

1 **teaspoon ground cinnamon**

⅔ **cup hazelnuts, toasted and finely chopped**

4 **ounces milk chocolate, chopped**

1. Thaw the pastry sheets at room temperature for 40 minutes or until they're easy to handle. Heat the oven to 375°F. Lightly grease or line 2 baking sheets with parchment paper.

2. Stir the sugar, coffee mix and cinnamon in a small bowl. Sprinkle ¼ **cup** sugar mixture onto a work surface. Unfold **1** pastry sheet onto the sugar mixture. Sprinkle with ¼ **cup** sugar mixture. Roll the pastry sheet into a 12×10-inch rectangle. Sprinkle with ⅓ **cup** nuts. Gently press the nuts into the pastry with a rolling pin. Cut the pastry into **4** (12×2½-inch) strips. Cut **each** strip into **4** (3-inch) pieces. Cut **each** piece diagonally in half into **2** triangles, making **32** triangles. Starting at the wide side, roll the triangles up to make a crescent

KITCHEN TIP:
Cookies can be prepared through step 3, then frozen for up to 3 months. Reheat in a 300°F. oven for about 5 minutes or until the cookies are crisp. Let cool on a wire rack and drizzle with the melted chocolate just before serving.

shape. Place the pastries pointed-side down on a baking sheet. Repeat with the remaining pastry sheet, sugar mixture and nuts.

3. Bake for 15 minutes or until the pastries are golden. Remove the pastries from the baking sheets and cool on wire racks.

4. Place the chocolate into a microwavable bowl. Microwave on HIGH for about 30 seconds. Stir until the chocolate is melted and smooth. Drizzle the chocolate over the cookies. Cookies can be stored in an airtight container for up to 1 week.

THAW TIME: 40 minutes

PREP TIME: 20 minutes

BAKE TIME: 15 minutes

COOL TIME: 30 minutes

CHOCOLATE-COFFEE NAPOLEONS

MAKES 6 NAPOLEONS

1 sheet (half of 17-ounce package) frozen puff pastry dough

1 tablespoon instant coffee granules

¼ cup warm water

1 package (4-serving size) chocolate instant pudding and pie filling mix

1¾ cups whole milk plus 1 teaspoon, divided

3 tablespoons powdered sugar

2 tablespoons bittersweet or semisweet chocolate chips

1. Thaw puff pastry sheet according to package directions. Dissolve coffee granules in water in small bowl; set aside.

2. Combine pudding mix, 1¾ cups milk and coffee in medium bowl; mix according to package directions. Cover and refrigerate until needed.

3. Preheat oven to 400°F. Line large baking sheet with parchment paper. Unfold pastry sheet; cut into three strips along fold marks. Cut each strip crosswise into thirds, forming nine squares total. Place pastry squares on prepared baking sheet. Bake 12 to 15 minutes or until puffed and golden brown. Remove to wire rack to cool completely.

4. Blend powdered sugar and remaining 1 teaspoon milk in small bowl until smooth. Cut each pastry square in half crosswise with serrated knife to form 18 pieces total. Spread powdered sugar icing over tops of six pastry pieces.

5. Place chocolate chips in small resealable food storage bag. Microwave on MEDIUM (50%) 30 seconds or until melted. Cut small piece off one corner of bag; drizzle over iced pastry pieces. Place in refrigerator while assembling napoleons.

6. Spoon about 2 tablespoons pudding mixture over each of six pastry pieces; layer with remaining six pastry pieces and pudding mixture. Top with iced pastry pieces. Refrigerate until ready to serve.

EUROPEAN MOCHA FUDGE CAKE

MAKES 10 TO 12 SERVINGS

1¼ cups (2½ sticks) butter or margarine

¾ cup HERSHEY'S SPECIAL DARK® Cocoa

4 eggs

¼ teaspoon salt

1 teaspoon vanilla extract

2 cups sugar

1 cup all-purpose flour

1 cup finely chopped pecans

Creamy Coffee Filling (page 95)

Chocolate curls (optional)

1. Heat oven to 350°F. Butter bottom and sides of two 9-inch round baking pans. Line bottoms with wax paper; butter paper.

2. Melt butter in small saucepan; remove from heat. Add cocoa, stirring until blended; cool slightly. Beat eggs in large bowl until foamy; add salt and vanilla. Gradually add sugar, beating well. Add cooled chocolate mixture; blend thoroughly. Fold in flour. Stir in pecans. Pour mixture into prepared pans.

3. Bake 20 to 25 minutes or until wooden pick inserted in center comes out clean. Do not overbake. Cool 5 minutes; remove from pans to wire racks. Carefully peel off paper. Cool completely. Spread Creamy Coffee Filling between layers, over top and sides of cake. Garnish with chocolate curls, if desired. Refrigerate 1 hour or longer before serving. Cover leftover cake; store in refrigerator.

MAKE AHEAD DIRECTIONS: Cooled cake may be wrapped and frozen up to 4 weeks; thaw before filling and frosting.

CREAMY COFFEE FILLING

1½ cups cold whipping
   cream

⅓ cup packed light
   brown sugar

2 teaspoons powdered
   instant coffee

Combine all ingredients; stir until instant coffee is almost dissolved. Beat until stiff. Makes about 3 cups filling.

CHOCOLATE CAPPUCCINO CAKE

MAKES 12 SERVINGS

REYNOLDS®
Parchment Paper

1 package (about 18 ounces) chocolate cake mix

¼ cup instant coffee, divided

2 teaspoons hot water

1 container (16 ounces) ready-to-spread cream cheese frosting

½ cup semi-sweet chocolate chips

2 teaspoons vegetable oil

Fresh raspberries (optional)

Preheat oven to 350°F. Line a 13×9×2-inch baking pan with REYNOLDS Parchment Paper, extending paper up sides of pan; set aside. Prepare cake mix following package directions, adding 2 tablespoons instant coffee before mixing. Spoon cake batter into parchment paper-lined baking pan.

Bake 29 to 34 minutes or until wooden pick inserted in center comes out clean. Cool. Invert cake onto a platter; remove parchment paper.

Dissolve remaining instant coffee in hot water. Stir frosting into coffee mixture until smooth. Frost cake. Microwave chocolate chips and oil on HIGH (100%) power in a small microwave-safe dish, 1 to 1½ minutes, stirring once, until chocolate is melted. Drizzle melted chocolate over frosted cake. Let stand until chocolate sets. Cut into 12 squares. Garnish with fresh raspberries, if desired.

PREP TIME: 10 minutes

COOK TIME: 29 minutes

COFFEE TOFFEE BISCOTTINI

MAKES 48 BISCOTTINI

- 2½ cups all-purpose flour
- 1 teaspoon baking powder
- ½ teaspoon salt
- 1 cup (2 sticks) unsalted butter
- 2 teaspoons freeze-dried coffee powder
- ½ cup granulated sugar
- ⅓ cup packed light brown sugar
- 2 large eggs
- ½ cup coarsely chopped dark chocolate-covered almonds
- 1 cup milk chocolate toffee bits

1. Line large baking sheet with parchment paper; set aside. Combine flour, baking powder and salt in medium bowl; mix well.

2. Beat butter and coffee powder in large bowl with electric mixer until light and fluffy. Add sugars; continue beating until light. Scrape down bowl. Add eggs, one at a time; mix well. Scrape down bowl. Add flour mixture, ½ cup at a time, beating well after each addition. Add almonds and toffee bits; mix only until blended. *Do not overmix.*

3. Arrange dough in 2 (12×2½-inch) strips on prepared baking sheet; gently pat to smooth top. Refrigerate 3 to 4 hours.

4. Preheat oven to 350°F. Bake strips 25 to 30 minutes or until light golden brown and firm. Remove from oven.

5. *Reduce oven temperature to 325°F.* Cool strips 10 minutes. With serrated knife, cut each strip into 1-inch-thick slices; cut each slice in half. Arrange pieces on baking sheet, cut-side up. Bake 15 minutes or until lightly browned. Cool 5 minutes; turn pieces over and bake 15 minutes or until lightly browned. Cool completely.

ESPRESSO GELATO

MAKES ABOUT 5 CUPS

2½ cups whole milk

1 cup whipping cream

¾ cup very coarsely ground espresso or Italian roast coffee beans

1 cup sugar

3 egg yolks

1 tablespoon plus 2 teaspoons cornstarch

1 teaspoon vanilla

1 cup mini semisweet chocolate chips

1. Heat milk, cream and espresso beans in heavy-bottomed medium saucepan over medium heat until bubbles form around edges of liquid. Remove from heat and let steep 10 minutes.

2. Whisk sugar, egg yolks and cornstarch in large bowl to form thick paste. Gradually whisk in hot espresso mixture. Rinse saucepan. Pour cream mixture into saucepan. Cook over medium heat, whisking constantly, being sure to reach into corners of saucepan, until mixture is barely simmering (cornstarch will prevent curdling). Strain through fine wire sieve (or standard sieve lined with moistened and wrung-out cheesecloth) into heatproof medium bowl. Stir in vanilla. Refrigerate 2 hours or until chilled.

3. Pour into frozen ice cream maker bowl. Fit frozen ice cream bowl and dasher on stand mixer. Turn mixer to stir setting and pour in cream mixture; stir on low 25 minutes or until the mixture is the consistency of soft-serve ice cream. Mix in chocolate chips.

4. Remove ice cream to freezer containers. Freeze 2 hours or until firm.

MINI MEXICAN COFFEE POPS

MAKES ABOUT 32 POPS

¼ cup ground dark roast coffee

2 (3-inch) cinnamon sticks, broken into pieces

2 cups water

1½ teaspoons sugar

⅓ cup cinnamon half-and-half*

½ teaspoon vanilla

Ice cube trays

Picks or mini pop sticks

You may use any flavor half-and-half or milk.

1. Place coffee and cinnamon sticks in filter basket of coffee maker. Add water to coffee maker and brew according to manufacturer's directions.

2. Remove coffee from heat. Stir in sugar until dissolved. Cool to room temperature, about 1 hour.

3. Add half-and-half and vanilla to cooled coffee. Pour mixture into ice cube trays. Freeze 2 hours.

4. Insert picks. Freeze 4 to 6 hours or until firm.

5. To remove pops from trays, place bottoms of ice cube trays under warm running water until loosened. Press firmly on bottoms to release. (Do not twist or pull picks.)

NANCY'S TIRAMISÙ

MAKES 12 SERVINGS

6 **egg yolks**

1¼ **cups sugar**

1½ **cups mascarpone cheese***

1¾ **cups whipping cream, beaten to soft peaks**

1¾ **cups cold espresso or strong brewed coffee**

3 **tablespoons brandy**

3 **tablespoons grappa (optional)**

4 **packages (3 ounces each) ladyfingers**

2 **tablespoons unsweetened cocoa powder**

Mascarpone cheese is an Italian soft cheese (similar to cream cheese) that is a traditional ingredient in tiramisù. Look for it in the specialty cheese section of the supermarket.

1. Beat egg yolks and sugar in small bowl with electric mixer at medium-high speed until pale yellow. Place in top of double boiler over simmering water. Cook, stirring constantly, 10 minutes. Combine yolk mixture and mascarpone cheese in large bowl; beat with electric mixer at low speed until well blended and fluffy. Fold in whipped cream. Set aside.

2. Combine espresso, brandy and grappa, if desired, in medium bowl. Dip 24 ladyfingers individually into espresso mixture and arrange side by side in single layer in 13×9-inch baking dish. (Dip ladyfingers into mixture quickly or they will absorb too much liquid and fall apart.)

3. Spread half of mascarpone mixture over ladyfinger layer. Sift 1 tablespoon cocoa over mascarpone layer. Repeat with another layer of 24 ladyfingers dipped in espresso mixture. Cover with remaining mascarpone mixture. Sift remaining 1 tablespoon cocoa over top.

4. Refrigerate at least 4 hours or overnight before serving.

SWEDISH LIMPA BREAD

MAKES 1 LOAF

1¾ to 2 cups all-purpose flour, divided

½ cup rye flour

1 package (¼ ounce) active dry yeast

1 tablespoon sugar

1½ teaspoons grated orange peel

1 teaspoon salt

½ teaspoon whole fennel seeds, crushed

½ teaspoon caraway seeds, crushed

¾ cup plus 4 teaspoons water, divided

4 tablespoons molasses, divided

2 tablespoons butter

1 teaspoon instant coffee granules

¼ teaspoon whole fennel seeds

¼ teaspoon whole caraway seeds

1. Combine 1½ cups all-purpose flour, rye flour, yeast, sugar, orange peel, salt and crushed fennel and caraway seeds in large bowl. Heat ¾ cup water, 3 tablespoons molasses and butter in small saucepan over low heat until temperature reaches 120° to 130°F. Stir in coffee granules. Stir water mixture into flour mixture with rubber spatula to form soft but sticky dough. Gradually add more all-purpose flour to form rough dough.

2. Turn out dough onto lightly floured surface. Knead 2 minutes or until soft dough forms, gradually add remaining all-purpose flour to prevent sticking, if necessary. Cover with inverted bowl; let rest 5 minutes. Continue kneading 5 to 8 minutes or until smooth and elastic. Shape dough into ball; place in large greased bowl. Turn to coat. Loosely cover with lightly greased sheet of plastic wrap. Let rise in warm place 75 minutes or until almost doubled in bulk.

3. Punch down dough. Grease 8½×4½-inch loaf pan. Roll dough into 12×7-inch rectangle. Starting with one short end, roll up tightly, jelly-roll style. Pinch seams and ends to seal. Place seam-side down in prepared pan. Cover loosely with plastic wrap. Let rise in warm place 1 hour or until doubled in bulk.

4. Preheat oven to 350°F. Stir remaining 1 tablespoon molasses and 4 teaspoons water in small bowl; set aside. Uncover loaf; make three diagonal slashes on top of dough using sharp knife. Bake 40 to 45 minutes or until loaf sounds hollow when tapped. Brush top with molasses mixture and sprinkle with whole fennel and caraway seeds halfway through baking time. Brush again with molasses mixture about 10 minutes before removing loaf from oven. Cool in pan on wire rack 5 minutes. Remove from pan. Cool completely on wire rack.

COOKIES WITH COFFEE

MOCHA CRINKLES

MAKES ABOUT 6 DOZEN COOKIES

- **1⅓ cups packed light brown sugar**
- **½ cup vegetable oil**
- **¼ cup sour cream**
- **1 egg**
- **1 teaspoon vanilla**
- **1¾ cups all-purpose flour**
- **¾ cup unsweetened cocoa powder**
- **2 teaspoons instant coffee granules**
- **1 teaspoon baking soda**
- **¼ teaspoon salt**
- **⅛ teaspoon black pepper**
- **½ cup powdered sugar**

1. Beat brown sugar and oil in large bowl with electric mixer at medium speed until well blended. Add sour cream, egg and vanilla; beat until well blended. Combine flour, cocoa, coffee granules, baking soda, salt and pepper in medium bowl; mix well. Beat into brown sugar mixture until well blended. Cover; refrigerate 3 to 4 hours.

2. Preheat oven to 350°F. Place powdered sugar in shallow bowl. Shape dough into 1-inch balls; roll in powdered sugar. Place 2 inches apart on ungreased cookie sheets.

3. Bake 10 to 12 minutes or until tops of cookies are firm. *Do not overbake.* Remove to wire racks; cool completely.

CAPPUCCINO SPICE COOKIES

MAKES ABOUT 3½ DOZEN COOKIES

2½ teaspoons instant coffee granules

1 tablespoon boiling water

2⅔ cups all-purpose flour

1 teaspoon baking soda

¾ teaspoon ground cinnamon

½ teaspoon salt

¼ teaspoon ground nutmeg or ground cloves

1 cup (2 sticks) butter, softened

1 cup packed light brown sugar

½ cup granulated sugar

2 eggs

1 teaspoon vanilla

1½ packages (12 ounces each) bittersweet or semisweet chocolate chips

1. Preheat oven to 375°F. Dissolve coffee granules in boiling water in small bowl.

2. Combine flour, baking soda, cinnamon, salt and nutmeg in medium bowl. Beat butter, brown sugar and granulated sugar in large bowl with electric mixer at medium speed until light and fluffy. Add eggs, coffee mixture and vanilla; beat until well blended. Gradually add flour mixture to butter mixture, beating at low speed until well blended. Stir in chocolate chips.

3. Drop dough by rounded tablespoonfuls 2 inches apart onto ungreased cookie sheets. Bake 8 to 10 minutes or until set. Cool on cookie sheets 1 minute. Remove to wire racks; cool completely.

CAPPUCCINO SPICE MINIS: For smaller cookies, prepare dough as directed above. Drop dough by rounded teaspoonfuls 2 inches apart onto ungreased cookie sheets. Bake 7 minutes or until set. Makes about 7 dozen mini cookies.

SUPER-EASY MOCHA ICED CHOCOLATE CHIP COOKIES

MAKES 2 DOZEN COOKIES

1 **package (16.5 ounces) NESTLÉ® TOLL HOUSE® Refrigerated Chocolate Chip Cookie Bar Dough**

1 **teaspoon NESCAFÉ® TASTER'S CHOICE® House Blend 100% Pure Instant Coffee Granules**

1 **teaspoon vanilla extract**

1 **package (8 ounces) cream cheese, softened**

⅓ **cup sifted powdered sugar**

1 **tablespoon NESTLÉ® TOLL HOUSE® Baking Cocoa**

BAKE cookies according to package directions; cool completely.

COMBINE coffee granules and vanilla extract in small bowl. Beat cream cheese in another small bowl until fluffy. Beat in powdered sugar, cocoa and coffee-vanilla mixture until well blended. Spread cookies with frosting. Store tightly covered in refrigerator.

PREP TIME: 5 minutes

BAKING TIME: 20 minutes

DAD'S GINGER MOLASSES COOKIES

MAKES ABOUT 4 DOZEN COOKIES

1 **cup shortening**

1 **cup granulated sugar**

1 **tablespoon baking soda**

2 **teaspoons ground ginger**

2 **teaspoons ground cinnamon**

1 **teaspoon ground cloves**

½ **teaspoon salt**

1 **cup molasses**

⅔ **cup double-strength instant coffee***

1 **egg**

4¾ **cups all-purpose flour**

To prepare double-strength coffee, follow instructions for instant coffee but use twice the recommended amount of instant coffee granules.

1. Preheat oven to 350°F. Lightly grease cookie sheets.

2. Beat shortening and sugar in large bowl with electric mixer at medium speed until creamy. Beat in baking soda, ginger, cinnamon, cloves and salt until well blended. Add molasses, coffee and egg, beating well after each addition. Gradually add flour, beating on low speed just until blended.

3. Drop dough by rounded tablespoonfuls 2 inches apart on prepared cookie sheets. Bake 12 to 15 minutes or until cookies are set but not browned. Cool on cookie sheets 1 minute. Remove to wire racks; cool completely.

ESPRESSO WHOOPIE PIES

MAKES 20 WHOOPIE PIES

Cookies

1⅔ cups all-purpose flour

1½ teaspoons baking soda

½ teaspoon salt

¾ cup hot coffee

⅔ cup unsweetened cocoa powder

2 tablespoons instant espresso powder

1 cup granulated sugar

½ cup (1 stick) unsalted butter, softened

1 egg

1½ teaspoons vanilla

Filling

2 cups powdered sugar

¾ cup (1½ sticks) butter, softened

1 tablespoon instant espresso powder dissolved in 2 tablespoons hot water

1½ teaspoons vanilla

1. For cookies, preheat oven to 350°F. Line two cookie sheets with parchment paper. Sift flour, baking soda and salt into medium bowl. Whisk coffee, cocoa and espresso powder in 2-cup measure until blended; cool to room temperature.

2. Beat granulated sugar and ½ cup butter in large bowl with electric mixer at medium speed 5 minutes or until light and fluffy. Beat in egg and 1½ teaspoons vanilla. Add half of flour mixture and half of coffee mixture; beat just until blended. Beat in remaining flour mixture and coffee mixture until smooth. Drop rounded tablespoonfuls of batter 2 inches apart onto prepared cookie sheets.

3. Bake 10 to 12 minutes or until cookies spring back when lightly touched. Cool 2 minutes on cookie sheets. Remove to wire racks; cool completely.

4. For filling, beat powdered sugar and ¾ cup butter in large bowl with electric mixer at medium speed 5 minutes or until light and fluffy. Add espresso mixture and 1½ teaspoons vanilla; beat until smooth.

5. Pipe or spread 2 tablespoons filling on flat side of half of cookies; top with remaining cookies.

BROWNIE COOKIES

MAKES 5 TO 6 DOZEN COOKIES

2½ cups all-purpose flour

⅓ cup unsweetened cocoa powder

1 teaspoon baking soda

1 teaspoon baking powder

1 teaspoon salt

1 cup granulated sugar

¾ cup packed brown sugar

½ cup (1 stick) butter, softened

¼ cup sour cream

1 tablespoon instant coffee granules, dissolved in 2 tablespoons hot water

2 eggs

1½ cups semisweet chocolate chips

1. Preheat oven to 325°F. Combine flour, cocoa, baking soda, baking powder and salt in medium bowl.

2. Beat granulated sugar, brown sugar, butter, sour cream and coffee mixture in large bowl with electric mixer at medium speed until creamy. Add eggs, one at a time, beating well after each addition until batter is light and fluffy.

3. Gradually add flour mixture to butter mixture, beating at low speed until just blended. Beat at medium speed 1 minute or until well blended. Stir in chocolate chips.

4. Drop dough by rounded tablespoonfuls onto ungreased cookie sheets. Bake 9 to 11 minutes or until slight imprint remains when pressed with finger. Cool on cookie sheets 3 minutes; remove to wire racks to cool completely.

MOCHA CHOCOLATE CHIP COOKIES

MAKES ABOUT 5 DOZEN COOKIES

2½ cups all-purpose flour

1 teaspoon salt

1 teaspoon baking soda

1 teaspoon ground cinnamon

1 cup (2 sticks) butter or margarine, softened

1 cup packed light brown sugar

½ cup granulated sugar

2 tablespoons HERSHEY'S SPECIAL DARK® Syrup

1½ teaspoons vanilla extract

2 eggs

1½ teaspoons powdered instant coffee or espresso, dissolved in 1 teaspoon hot water

2 cups (12-ounce package) HERSHEY'S SPECIAL DARK® Chocolate Chips

1½ cups chopped pecans

1. Heat oven to 350°F. Line cookie sheets with parchment paper.

2. Stir together flour, salt, baking soda and cinnamon. Beat butter, brown sugar, granulated sugar, chocolate syrup and vanilla in large bowl with mixer until creamy. Add eggs and coffee; beat well. Gradually add flour mixture, beating well. Stir in chocolate chips and pecans. Drop by rounded teaspoons about 2 inches apart onto prepared cookie sheets.

3. Bake 10 to 12 minutes or until lightly browned. Cool slightly; remove from cookie sheets to wire rack. Cool completely.

LATTE COOKIES

MAKES 6 DOZEN COOKIES

1¾ cups all-purpose flour

¼ cup unsweetened cocoa powder

1 tablespoon instant coffee granules

1 teaspoon baking soda

½ teaspoon ground cinnamon

½ cup (1 stick) butter, softened

½ cup packed dark brown sugar

¼ cup sour cream

1 egg

1 egg white

1 teaspoon vanilla

Powdered sugar

¼ cup chopped bittersweet chocolate

2 tablespoons half-and-half

1. Preheat oven to 350°F. Combine flour, cocoa, coffee granules, baking soda and cinnamon in large bowl; set aside.

2. Beat butter in large bowl with electric mixer at medium speed 30 seconds or until creamy. Beat in brown sugar and sour cream at medium-low speed until well blended. Add egg, egg white and vanilla; beat at low speed until well blended.

3. Gradually add flour mixture to butter mixture, beating at low speed until well blended.

4. Drop dough by level teaspoonfuls onto ungreased cookie sheets. Flatten cookies slightly with bottom of greased glass. Bake 6 minutes. Cool 5 minutes on cookie sheets. Remove to wire racks; cool completely.

5. Dust cookies with powdered sugar. For icing, heat chocolate and half-and-half in small saucepan over very low heat, stirring until chocolate is melted. Drizzle over cookies. Let stand until icing is firm.

PECAN PINWHEELS

MAKES ABOUT 5 DOZEN COOKIES

1 square (1 ounce) unsweetened chocolate

¾ cup packed brown sugar

½ cup (1 stick) butter, softened

1 egg

1 teaspoon vanilla

¼ teaspoon baking soda

1¾ cups all-purpose flour

½ cup chopped pecans

1 teaspoon instant espresso powder

1. Melt chocolate in small bowl over hot, not boiling, water; stir until smooth. Beat brown sugar, butter, egg, vanilla and baking soda in large bowl with electric mixer at medium speed until well blended. Stir in flour to make stiff dough. Remove half of dough to another large bowl. Blend pecans and espresso powder into one half of dough. Stir melted chocolate into remaining half of dough. Cover doughs; refrigerate 30 minutes.

2. Roll out coffee dough into 15×8-inch rectangle between two sheets of plastic wrap. Roll chocolate dough out to same dimensions between two additional sheets of plastic wrap. Remove top sheets of plastic wrap. Place coffee dough on top of chocolate dough. Remove remaining sheets of plastic wrap. Roll up firmly, jelly-roll fashion, starting with long side. Wrap in plastic wrap; freeze until firm enough to handle. (Dough can be frozen up to six weeks.)

3. Preheat oven to 350°F. Line cookie sheets with parchment paper or leave ungreased. Cut frozen dough into ¼-inch-thick slices; place 2 inches apart on prepared cookie sheets. Bake 9 to 12 minutes or until set. Remove to wire racks to cool.

CAPPUCCINO COOKIES

MAKES ABOUT 4 DOZEN COOKIES

1 package (about 18 ounces) devil's food cake mix

8 egg whites

¾ cup milk

1 tablespoon instant coffee granules

1 teaspoon ground cinnamon

Powdered sugar

1. Preheat oven to 400°F. Lightly spray cookie sheets with nonstick cooking spray.

2. Mix cake mix, egg whites, milk, coffee granules and cinnamon in medium bowl with spatula until well blended. Drop dough by rounded teaspoonfuls onto prepared cookie sheets.

3. Bake 5 minutes or until centers are set. Cool on cookie sheets 1 minute. Remove to wire racks; cool completely. Sprinkle with powdered sugar.

CHOCOLATE DROPS

MAKES 3 DOZEN COOKIES

1 (3-ounce) coffee-flavored chocolate bar*

½ cup (1 stick) plus 1 tablespoon unsalted butter, softened

½ cup powdered sugar

1 teaspoon instant coffee granules

¼ teaspoon salt

2 tablespoons unsweetened cocoa

1 cup all-purpose flour

Granulated sugar

Purchase a chocolate bar with coffee flavoring, not a cream-filled coffee center.

1. Preheat oven to 325°F. Line two cookie sheets with parchment paper. Break chocolate bar into 36 small pieces; chill.

2. Beat butter, powdered sugar, coffee granules and salt with electric mixer at medium-high speed. Stir in cocoa. Add flour, ¼ cup at a time, beating at medium speed until dough comes together.

3. Shape rounded teaspoonfuls of dough into 36 balls. Place on prepared cookie sheets 1½ inches apart. Flatten cookies to ⅓-inch thickness with glass dipped in granulated sugar. Bake 12 to 14 minutes or until cookies are set.

4. Remove cookies from oven and top each with chocolate piece. Let chocolate soften on hot cookies. When chocolate looks glossy spread over cookies with back of spoon.

COOKIES WITH COFFEE

NO-BAKE COOKIE BALLS

MAKES ABOUT 4 DOZEN

1¾ cups chocolate graham cracker crumbs (9 to 11 crackers)

1½ cups (8 ounces) chocolate-covered coffee beans, coarsely chopped

1 cup finely chopped walnuts

½ cup plus 1 teaspoon instant espresso powder

¼ teaspoon salt

¾ cup dark corn syrup

1 teaspoon vanilla

½ cup powdered sugar

1. Combine graham cracker crumbs, coffee beans, walnuts, 1 teaspoon espresso powder and salt in large bowl; mix well.

2. Stir in corn syrup and vanilla. Knead by hand until mixture comes together. Shape into 1-inch balls.

3. Spread powdered sugar on small baking sheet; roll half of balls in sugar to coat. Spread remaining ½ cup espresso powder on separate small baking sheet; roll remaining half of balls in espresso powder to coat.

TIP: To make cookie crumbs, place cookies in a food processor; process until finely ground. Or, place cookies in resealable food storage bag, and use rolling pin to crush cookies into fine crumbs.

CAPPUCCINO COOKIES

MAKES ABOUT 5 DOZEN COOKIES

1 **cup (2 sticks) butter, softened**

2 **cups packed brown sugar**

2 **tablespoons milk**

2 **tablespoons instant coffee granules**

2 **eggs**

1 **teaspoon rum extract**

½ **teaspoon vanilla**

4 **cups all-purpose flour**

1 **teaspoon baking powder**

½ **teaspoon ground nutmeg**

¼ **teaspoon salt**

Semisweet chocolate, melted

1. Beat butter in large bowl with electric mixer at medium speed until smooth. Add brown sugar; beat until well blended.

2. Heat milk in small saucepan over low heat; add coffee granules, stirring to dissolve. Add milk mixture, eggs, rum extract and vanilla to butter mixture. Beat at medium speed until well blended.

3. Combine flour, baking powder, nutmeg and salt in large bowl. Gradually add flour mixture to butter mixture, beating at low speed after each addition until blended.

4. Shape dough into two (2 inches in diameter and 8 inches long) logs. (Dough will be soft; sprinkle lightly with flour if too sticky to handle.)

5. Preheat oven to 350°F. Grease cookie sheets. Cut logs into ¼-inch-thick slices; place 1 inch apart on cookie sheets. (Keep unbaked logs and sliced cookies chilled until ready to bake.)

6. Bake 10 to 12 minutes or until edges are lightly browned. Remove to wire racks to cool completely. Dip each cookie into melted chocolate, coating 1 inch up sides. Remove to wire racks or waxed paper; let stand at room temperature 40 minutes or until chocolate is set. Store in airtight container.

MOCHA MADNESS

MAKES 3 DOZEN COOKIES

½ cup (1 stick) unsalted butter, softened

½ cup packed light brown sugar

¼ cup granulated sugar

1 egg

1 teaspoon vanilla

1 cup all-purpose flour

½ teaspoon salt

½ teaspoon baking soda

½ cup chopped pecans

1 bar (3 ounces) coffee-flavored chocolate, finely chopped

Latte Glaze (recipe follows)

1. Preheat oven to 350°F. Lightly grease cookie sheets.

2. Beat butter and sugars in large bowl with electric mixer at medium speed until creamy. Add egg and vanilla; beat until well blended, scraping down side of bowl once. Combine flour, salt and baking soda in small bowl. Gradually add flour mixture to butter mixture, beating until well blended. Stir in pecans and chocolate.

3. Drop dough by tablespoonfuls 3 inches apart onto cookie sheets. Bake 10 to 12 minutes or until set and lightly browned. Cool 5 minutes on cookie sheets. Remove to wire racks to cool completely.

4. Prepare Latte Glaze; drizzle over cookies. Let stand 30 minutes or until set.

LATTE GLAZE

MAKES ABOUT ½ CUP

1 teaspoon freeze-dried or instant coffee granules

1 to 2 tablespoons half-and-half

⅛ teaspoon salt

½ cup powdered sugar

Combine coffee granules, 1 tablespoon half-and-half and salt in small microwavable bowl. Microwave on HIGH 15 seconds or until coffee is dissolved. Stir in powdered sugar until smooth. If necessary, stir in remaining half-and-half by teaspoons until desired glaze consistency is reached.

CHEWY BROWNIE COOKIES

MAKES 2 DOZEN COOKIES

1 cup all-purpose flour

¼ teaspoon baking soda

¼ cup (½ stick) butter

⅔ cup granulated sugar

⅓ cup unsweetened cocoa powder

¼ cup packed brown sugar

1½ teaspoons instant coffee granules

¼ cup buttermilk

1 teaspoon vanilla

2 tablespoons powdered sugar

1. Combine flour and baking soda in small bowl; mix well. Melt butter in medium saucepan; remove from heat. Stir in granulated sugar, cocoa, brown sugar and coffee granules until well blended. Stir in buttermilk and vanilla. Stir in flour mixture just until combined. Remove to medium bowl. Cover; refrigerate 1 hour. (Dough will be stiff.)

2. Preheat oven to 350°F. Spray cookie sheets with nonstick cooking spray or line with parchment paper. Drop dough by rounded teaspoonfuls onto prepared cookie sheets.

3. Bake 10 to 11 minutes or until edges are firm. Cool on cookie sheets 2 minutes. Remove to wire racks; cool completely. Sprinkle with powdered sugar just before serving.

NO-BAKE COFFEE BEAN COOKIES

MAKES ABOUT 3 DOZEN COOKIES

1 **package (9 ounces) chocolate wafer cookies**

⅓ **cup light corn syrup**

⅓ **cup coffee-flavored liqueur**

1 **cup finely chopped walnuts, toasted***

¾ **cup powdered sugar**

3 **tablespoons unsweetened cocoa powder**

Chocolate-covered coffee beans

To toast walnuts, spread in single layer on baking sheet. Toast in preheated 350°F oven 6 to 8 minutes or until golden brown, stirring frequently.

1. Break half of cookies in half; place in food processor. Process using on/off pulses until fine crumbs form. Transfer to small bowl. Repeat with remaining cookies. Combine corn syrup and liqueur in medium bowl; stir until well blended. Stir in crumbs and walnuts until well blended.

2. Combine powdered sugar and cocoa in small bowl; stir until well blended. Add ½ cup cocoa mixture to cookie crumb mixture; stir until blended. Reserve remaining cocoa mixture for coating.

3. Shape dough into 1-inch balls with greased hands; place on large baking sheets. Cover; refrigerate at least 3 hours or up to three days before serving.

4. Roll each ball in reserved cocoa mixture to coat; remove to large serving plate. Top each cookie with chocolate-covered coffee bean. Serve cold or at room temperature.

INDEX

INDEX

INDEX

INDEX

ACKNOWLEDGMENTS

The publisher would like to thank the companies and organizations listed below
for the use of their recipes and photographs in this publication.

California Dried Plum Board

Campbell Soup Company

Cream of Wheat® Cereal

Dole Food Company, Inc.

The Hershey Company

Nestlé USA

The Quaker® Oatmeal Kitchens

Recipes courtesy of Reynolds Kitchens

METRIC CONVERSION CHART

VOLUME MEASUREMENTS (dry)

1/8 teaspoon = 0.5 mL
1/4 teaspoon = 1 mL
1/2 teaspoon = 2 mL
3/4 teaspoon = 4 mL
1 teaspoon = 5 mL
1 tablespoon = 15 mL
2 tablespoons = 30 mL
1/4 cup = 60 mL
1/3 cup = 75 mL
1/2 cup = 125 mL
2/3 cup = 150 mL
3/4 cup = 175 mL
1 cup = 250 mL
2 cups = 1 pint = 500 mL
3 cups = 750 mL
4 cups = 1 quart = 1 L

VOLUME MEASUREMENTS (fluid)

1 fluid ounce (2 tablespoons) = 30 mL
4 fluid ounces (1/2 cup) = 125 mL
8 fluid ounces (1 cup) = 250 mL
12 fluid ounces (1 1/2 cups) = 375 mL
16 fluid ounces (2 cups) = 500 mL

WEIGHTS (mass)

1/2 ounce = 15 g
1 ounce = 30 g
3 ounces = 90 g
4 ounces = 120 g
8 ounces = 225 g
10 ounces = 285 g
12 ounces = 360 g
16 ounces = 1 pound = 450 g

DIMENSIONS

1/16 inch = 2 mm
1/8 inch = 3 mm
1/4 inch = 6 mm
1/2 inch = 1.5 cm
3/4 inch = 2 cm
1 inch = 2.5 cm

OVEN TEMPERATURES

250°F = 120°C
275°F = 140°C
300°F = 150°C
325°F = 160°C
350°F = 180°C
375°F = 190°C
400°F = 200°C
425°F = 220°C
450°F = 230°C

BAKING PAN SIZES

Utensil	Size in Inches/Quarts	Metric Volume	Size in Centimeters
Baking or Cake Pan (square or rectangular)	8×8×2	2 L	20×20×5
	9×9×2	2.5 L	23×23×5
	12×8×2	3 L	30×20×5
	13×9×2	3.5 L	33×23×5
Loaf Pan	8×4×3	1.5 L	20×10×7
	9×5×3	2 L	23×13×7
Round Layer Cake Pan	8×1½	1.2 L	20×4
	9×1½	1.5 L	23×4
Pie Plate	8×1¼	750 mL	20×3
	9×1¼	1 L	23×3
Baking Dish or Casserole	1 quart	1 L	—
	1½ quarts	1.5 L	—
	2 quarts	2 L	—